Children of the World

madhi
A Child of Egypt

By Muriel Nicolotti

BLACKBIRCH PRESS
An imprint of Thomson Gale, a part of The Thomson Corporation

Detroit • New York • San Francisco • San Diego • New Haven, Conn. • Waterville, Maine • London • Munich

© Éditions PEMF, 2000

First published by PEMF in France as *Madhi, enfant Égyptien*.

First published in North America in 2005 by Thomson Gale.

Thomson and Star Logo are trademarks and Gale and Blackbirch Press are registered trademarks used herein under license.

For more information, contact
Blackbirch Press
27500 Drake Rd.
Farmington Hills, MI 48331-3535
Or you can visit our Internet site at http://www.gale.com

ALL RIGHTS RESERVED.
No part of this work covered by the copyright hereon may be reproduced or used in any form or by any means—graphic, electronic, or mechanical, including photocopying, recording, taping, Web distribution or information storage retrieval systems—without the written permission of the publisher.

Every effort has been made to trace the owners of copyrighted material.

Photo Credits: All photos © Muriel Nicolotti except cover, page 1 CIRIC/Michel Gauvry; pages 6, 7, 9, 10 (top); 11, 17, 18, 19 François Goalec; pages 10 (bottom), 22, 23 (top left) Corel Corporation; Table of Contents collage: EXPLORER/Boutin (upper left); François Goalec (upper middle and right); Muriel Nicolotti (bottom left); CIRIC/Michel Gauvry (bottom middle); CIRIC/Pascal Deloche (bottom right)

LIBRARY OF CONGRESS CATALOGING-IN-PUBLICATION DATA

Nicolotti, Muriel.
  Madhi : a child of Egypt / by Muriel Nicolotti.
    p. cm. — (Children of the world)
  ISBN 1-4103-0288-1 (hard cover : alk. paper)
  1. Egypt—Juvenile literature. I. Title. II. Series: Children of the world (Blackbirch Press)

DT49.N5 2005
962.05'5--dc22
                                                              2005000703

Printed in the United States of America
10 9 8 7 6 5 4 3 2 1

Contents

Facts About Egypt 5
Cairo 6
Madhi's Village 8
Daily Life 10
The Village Festival 12
The Temple of Millions of Years 14
A Voyage on the Nile 16
Aswan 18
Abu Simbel 20
Hieroglyphs 22
Other Titles in the Series 24

Facts About Egypt

Agriculture:	cotton, rice, corn, wheat, beans, fruits, vegetables
Capital:	Cairo
Government:	republic
Industry:	textiles, food processing, tourism, chemicals, hydrocarbons, cement, metals
Land Area:	386,662 square miles (1,001,449 square kilometers)
Languages:	Arabic; English; French
Money:	the Egyptian pound
Natural Resources:	oil, natural gas, iron ore, phosphates, manganese, limestone, gypsum, talc, asbestos, lead, zinc
Population:	71,931,000
Religions:	Muslim (94 percent), Coptic Christian and other (6 percent)

Cairo

Cairo, which means "the victorious" in Arabic, is the capital of Egypt. With 6 million people, it is the largest city in Africa and in the Arab world.

Greater Cairo includes seven new cities. Thirteen million people live in Cairo. Five million of these are children.

The market is located in the old part of the city.

Cairo combines history and modernity. The Sphinx and the pyramids of Khafre, Menkaure, and Khufu are in Giza. Giza is a suburb of Cairo.

Children swim and play in the Nile.

The three pyramids of Giza are 5 miles (8 kilometers) from Cairo.

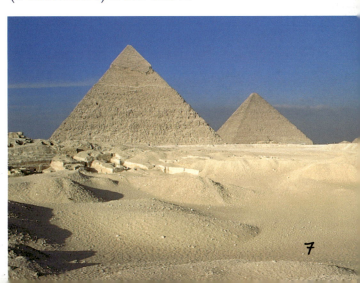

Madhi's Village

Madhi is nine years old. He lives on the banks of the Nile. His village is in the middle of the ruins of the ancient city of Thebes.

A peaceful street in Luxor.

In Madhi's village, between the houses, there are tombs that are more than 3,000 years old.

Daily Life

Tourists from around the world come to visit the city of Luxor. This city is 466 miles (750 kilometers) south of Cairo on the banks of the Nile. The people live peacefully among the ruins.

Because the school is not big enough for all the students to attend at the same time, some children attend in the morning from 8 A.M. to 1 P.M. and the rest from 1 P.M. to 6 P.M.

Classes are large—between 50 and 100 children in each class.

Above: The elementary school in Luxor.

The Village Festival

Each year, Madhi waits impatiently for the festival days in his village. There are merry-go-rounds and a snake charmer with a blue-eyed cobra.

The snake charmer.

There are also equestrian games. Riders gallop by on their spirited Arabian horses. They race past each other in a cloud of dust. Then their horses dance in front of the musicians.

Madhi is enchanted by this spectacle, deafened by the whinnies and the pounding of hooves.

Inset: A group of musicians.

Left: The horses make the dust fly.

13

The Temple of Millions of Years

Madhi likes to visit his older brother. He works on the archaeological site of Karnak, which was once linked to Luxor by an alley of sphinxes. The temple that Madhi likes best is the Temple of Millions of Years. The history of ancient Egypt is written on its walls.

Unfortunately, many temples have been destroyed or broken into and robbed.

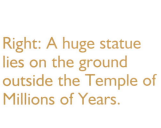

Right: A huge statue lies on the ground outside the Temple of Millions of Years.

Archaeologists from around the world live on the site at Karnak. They are working to preserve, reconstruct, or even discover tombs that are still hidden.

Madhi's brother works on the reconstruction of a temple. He works for French archaeologists.

Right: The team moves big blocks of sandstone. They rebuild the partially destroyed temple stone by stone.

Bottom: Three thousand years ago, the pharaoh Ramses II pushed his enemies, the Hittites, out of Egypt.

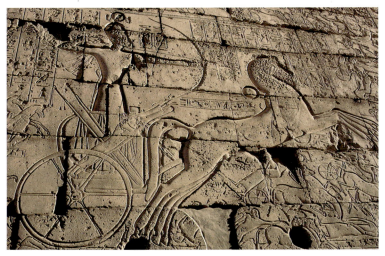

A Voyage on the Nile

This morning, Madhi and his father leave in a boat on the Nile. The sun has barely risen over the mountain. They are headed to the south of Egypt.

It will take several days in their felouk, or sailboat, to reach Aswan.

Left: Men fish on the Nile.

While they sail on the Nile, Madhi and his father meet other people on felouks and fishing boats. Boaters strike the water with their oars to drive fish into their nets.

A felouk is filled to capacity.

The trip is long. The felouk moves slowly. This allows time to admire the banks of the Nile and the magnificent scenery.

Aswan

The felouk gets close to Aswan. It is almost the end of the trip. Madhi sees the palm trees of the oasis.

His father has taken this trip to go to the camel market near Aswan. Traders come there to choose and buy animals that they will sell throughout North Africa.

Above: In the distance lies the city of Aswan.

Right: The tranquil banks of the Nile are seen from Aswan.

Above: The outdoor market at Aswan.

Left: The camel market at Aswan.

19

Abu Simbel

Madhi leaves Aswan to go south to Abu Simbel.

Because the Nile regularly flooded its banks, Egypt built a dam and created an artificial lake full of fish. Three thousand years ago, the ancient Egyptian pharaoh Ramses II carved a big temple into a mountain facing the Nile. But the rising lake waters threatened this extraordinary site. Condemned to be flooded, the two temples of Abu Simbel were saved by an international organization called UNESCO.

Cut into 1,036 blocks, some weighing 30 short tons (27 metric tons), the two temples were rebuilt against an artificial mountain 210 feet (64 meters) high.

The work took five years.

Egyptians and tourists are still able to visit and admire the temple of Ramses II.

The temple of Ramses II. The colossi, or big statues that represent the pharaoh sitting on his throne, are 65 feet (20 meters) high.

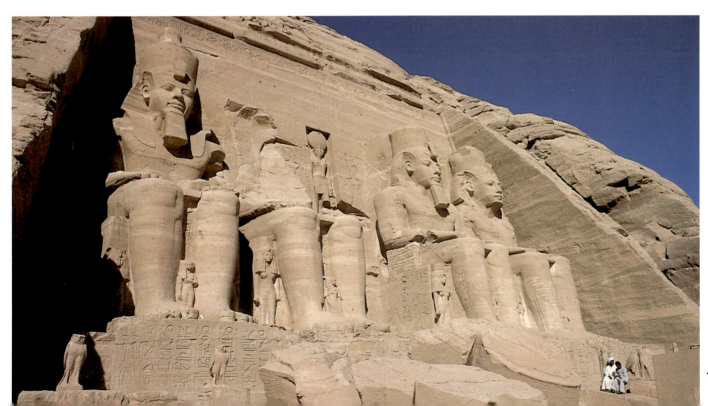

Hieroglyphs

The histories of the pharaohs and ancient Egypt are told in mysterious signs carved into the stone, called hieroglyphs.

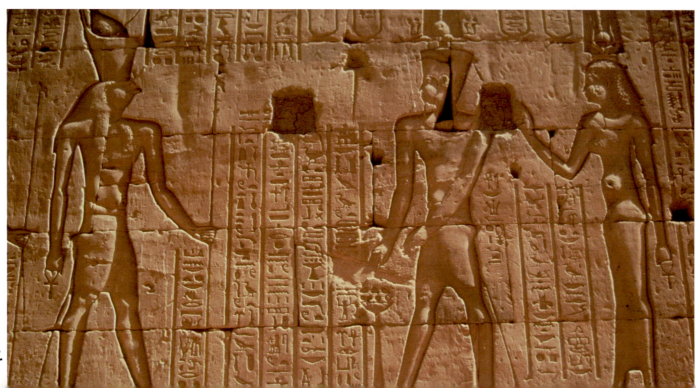

Right: Hieroglyphs appear on the side of a statue.

Other Books in the Series

Arafat: A Child of Tunisia
Asha: A Child of the Himalayas
Avinesh: A Child of the Ganges
Ballel: A Child of Senegal
Basha: A Hmong Child
Frederico: A Child of Brazil

Ituko: An Inuit Child
Kradji: A Child of Cambodia
Kuntai: A Masai Child
Leila: A Tuareg Child
Thanassis: A Child of Greece
Tomasino: A Child of Peru

962.05
NIC

Madhi.

16.32

30229012286752